SUMMER / BREAK

PREVIOUS BOOKS BY RICHIE MCCAFFERY

Poetry
Cairn, Nine Arches Press, 2014
Passport, Nine Arches Press, 2018

SUMMER / BREAK

RICHIE MCCAFFERY

Printed by imprintdigital
Upton Pyne, Exeter
www.digital.imprint.co.uk

Typesetting and cover design by The Book Typesetters
us@thebooktypesetters.com
07422 598 168
www.thebooktypesetters.com

Published by Shoestring Press
19 Devonshire Avenue, Beeston, Nottingham, NG9 1BS
(0115) 925 1827
www.shoestringpress.co.uk

First published 2022
© Copyright: Richie McCaffery
Cover painting: 'Harbour Wall' by Willie Rodger, © Willie Rodger Art Trust and reproduced with its permission

The moral right of the author has been asserted.

ISBN 978-1-915553-03-4

ACKNOWLEDGEMENTS

Heartfelt thanks are due to Helena Nelson, Chris Powici, Rory Watson, Matthew Stewart, Hamish Whyte and Walter Perrie for their invaluable help and support.

Some poems in this volume have previously appeared in two pamphlet collections: *First Hare* (Mariscat Press, 2020) and *Coping Stones* (Fras Publications, 2021).

In addition other poems have appeared online, or in print, at the following places: *Bad Lilies, Fras, The Friday Poem, Frogmore Papers, The High Window, Interpreter's House, Northwords Now, Poetry Salzburg Review, Wet Grain, Wild Court.*

CONTENTS

BREAK

OUT OF THE BLUE

She left me at the height of nesting season,
birds building while I was dismantling my home.

She left me as brambles we'd planted were fruiting,
their berries tart like the metal of front door keys.

She left me and I walked down the garden path
for the last time, all confettied with blossom,

the petals like plectrums as if one day
I might learn to make music from all this.

Summer

COPING STONES

All around the edge of the estate,
hand-hewn 18th century masonry
capping tall sandstone walls.

I remember seeing the foundations
and crypt of a medieval church
built from rubble of a Roman temple.

So it stands to reason that should
these high walls fall, we could salvage
the top stonework to make a home

where we would weather it out,
nothing would get to us
in our house of coping stones.

ANCHOR

We had a time cutting your hair in lockdown,
russet curls all over the patio – left
them for the birds and their nests
but it struck me that they all spelled
the initial of your first name, 'S' for 'Stef'

how you sometimes see that shape
on the side of old buildings, a wall anchor
securing a steel beam that gives a spine
to a weak edifice and how you in your way
go through my life, doing the same.

SANKOFA BIRD

Whenever there's a bird we don't
recognise in the back garden
we like to imagine it's a sankofa.

Once fed, watered and rested
it'll migrate way back in time
and fix a snag or nick in our past,

bring back a budding twig
from a tree felled and regretted
that now stands again.

We've no time to worry
if the bird we see is in fact
on its outward journey.

STEF

i.

To burn a candle for someone
is to wave the flag high for them
and many countries have only one.

I'm an adopter of single candlesticks,
Victorian brass batons, all along
the mantelpiece, lighting the evening.

It's only when I snuff them out
I notice there isn't much difference
between one candle and many

unlike the difference
between one candle and none.

ii.

Names, like the languages we speak,
were decided before we were born.
All we can do is tweak ours, make
few syllables mean more than many.

Here's a question: whoever decided
to call the house *semi-detached*,
not *semi-attached*? Your parents gave
you this name to come running to.

But they stopped speaking it too,
pushed you all the way abroad.
That's where you learned mine,
I incanted yours until you stayed.

GETTING WARMER

The ground of Hulne Park this morning's
so frosty cold it feels as if it's been baked.

Like that sensation, young and impatient
of putting your dirty hands under the tap
before the soapy basin is filled –

the water's scalding – but for a moment
you can't tell if it's hot or cold,
and you can only bathe in a mixture of both.

Alnwick's the tenth place I've lived
in my adult life. I'm toasty this winter day.

LE MERLE BLANC

Made in England, the *Blackbird*
fountain pen was also exported to Belgium
as *Le Merle Blanc* – white blackbird.

The one I write with was your grandfather's,
a gift for his first Holy Communion
and then for me, seven decades later.

Silenced by the war, its bladder burst,
holding in unwritten secrets.
Repaired, it writes in English instead.

We are the produce of one nation
packaged for another, and unlike
the politics of our times

this pen's gold beak of a nib
has such a beautiful flex to it.

NORTHUMBRIAN

i.

Northumberland is full of drystone
walls like petrified weirs.
I never know the territories they mark,
never saw them built or fixed.

I want us to be like one of these walls –
nothing between us, no mortar or cement,
slotted in perfectly together, lichens
awarded us like rosettes.

ii.

The Duke's selling off his farmland
to the developers,
and still there's nowhere
we seem to be able to live.

We move so much I sometimes
think we're stolen goods.
I helped you spot your first hare.
This fact seems important now.

iii.

You asked me why, in the village
and fields where I grew up,
there are large blue barrels –
They're pheasant feeders, I said.

You told me: *That's so kind!*
I hadn't the heart to speak the truth
and kill your desire to see good
always in the midst of bad.

Our love fattens itself daily
unaware of greater schemes at play.

CIRCADIAN RHYTHMS

after Donald Hall

Most diaries would have had it blank, that day.
We woke late, you fed the cat, I the birds
then we made breakfast together.

You had a shower, I had my bath.
We read, we worked from home, we went
for a walk to see the new fish pass on the river.

You cooked lunch, and I did dinner.
You spoke Flemish online with family.
I stuck to English on the phone with my mother.

The cat sat on each of our laps. We went
to bed together, both asleep within minutes.
It was one of the best days of my life.

CEDAR OF LEBANON

We walk all the way uphill through Wooler
to get to the giant Lebanese cedar—
I could be a pilgrim if it's a journey
to a special tree and nothing more.

You recall the great groves in Lebanon
as we stand under its huge prickly umbrella
gathering cones hard as green grenades
that we take away to try and grow elsewhere,

to be thrown into the future and explode
in mushroom clouds of resinous canopies
and I could be a soldier if it only involved
this task and nothing else.

LIGHTHOUSE

On our bedroom wall
a framed Victorian print
of a lighthouse in a tempest.

My penultimate view
before I look at you
and turn off the light.

It's drawn in such a way
to imply that the onlooker
is deep in the eye of the storm.

DOBBIN

The last painting my grandmother made,
1998, watercolour, Woolworths' frame.
A portrait of an old sorrel donkey.

Grandad said it looked like it was
about to be sent to the knackers' yard.
He didn't much like her 'daubs'.

She painted all her life but this
was the only one she tried to sell
at the annual Shipcote Art Society sale.

No-one wanted it so she brought it home
and gave it to me when I tried to buy it
to save her feelings.

I still have it, that spavined cuddy
with a bridle so big it nearly covers its face
and you can't see who's holding the reins.

After all these years, from wall to wall,
I still look at it standing there,
waiting for sugar lumps.

CAFÉ DE TROLLEKELDER

The pub of trolls on St Jacobs,
where my mother and I liked to go
when I lived in Ghent
to drink beers so dark and strong
the night always came too early.

Here she told me she'd been abused
as a child. At the same time the city
was laying tracks outside
for an extension to the tram,
connecting faraway places.

Her words drove into me like rivets
and I woke up early morning
to the sound of construction work
as if tomorrow was something
they were working on to improve.

SPORTS DAYS

While I was at school Mam was a cleaner there
after Dad lost his job at the Coal Board.

She'd been a guitar tech for world-famous bands
yet she traded it all in for our vague village life

where long-playing became long-suffering,
a heavy-metal head giving birth to an anaemic.

She worked three jobs and raised two of us.
I saw her once, during break, cleaning my classroom.

When I caught her eye she pulled down the blinds.
I never was embarrassed. She cleansed the place.

On mandatory sports day I always took pride
in taking my time and if someone fell down,

bloodied their knee I'd stop to help them back up.
She'd be there, cheering me on as I came last.

MR FLEET

We recognise each other at the same time –
Mr Fleet, my old geography teacher. He says
Time flies and our names come to each other
like a mnemonic, decades since we last met.

He's dressed for the weather, with binoculars,
but he'll not see a rarer bird on his walk than me.
He fires off big questions like I'm in an exam,
keen to map the lie of the land of my adult life.

He wants to talk more but I'm not sure
I've passed the test and his waiting wife
is used to this sort of thing, the once bright
meeting him dulled, and she's keen to get on.

BACK TO SCHOOL

Our family tradition, on the first day back
was to stand on the wall in front of our house
by an old millstone for a photograph.

The goal of the grind year upon year
was supposed to separate wheat from chaff
and I did eventually learn enough to know

that what I had been told all along
was a millstone is in fact an old knife
grinder's wheel and although my memory's

blunted after all these years, there were cuts
in childhood that were so sharp you never
felt them until the blood welled up years later

VENTRILOQUIST

Most of my peers threw their voices far,
shotguns for playboy dukes
the audience ran after like hunt dogs.

But I was a different kind of artist,
trained for years to plunge my voice
back down deep inside me, the runt

in a brick sack thrown down the well.
I am the best of my kind though there's
no applause. Just now a shopkeeper

asked me to repeat myself five times.
The way they close their eyes, lean in,
trying to hear the cries of dead
ancestors deep in the earth.

BEARINGS

When I was little and much more curious
one of the main things my parents drilled
into my head was if I ever got lost
I should just stay still until I was found.

Here I am in my mid-thirties, lost again
even though my location is clear.
I'm staying still in the hope
of being found for real.

WASTED

I meet an old friend in the street.
He's coked up and I'm drunk.
As we sway and spasm
we ask each other how we are.
Our answers are rehearsed:
we're good, things are good.

We're two ambulances
on blue lights and sirens
passing in opposite directions
on a busy highway
but still bothering to wave
to each other.

I walk away ashamed at how I feel
thinking of how sore and scabbed
my grandfather's legs were
as if nightly he had to kick himself
free from the clutches of death
to see another day.

WEEDING

I hated gardening, thought it futile
but that was before
we were ordered to stay at home.

A whole day spent weeding
and wondering what sort of genus
my lineage is made of –

the kind easily deracinated
or a tougher breed that sacrifices
its leaves and flowers when pulled
so that the roots remain.

NO FELLOW TRAVELLERS

'...those who are going nowhere can have no fellow travellers.' – C. S. Lewis

On our way back from the beach
we stop at the village graveyard
and find people we knew

whom we didn't think were dead
and still we've not got a good
word for many of them.

The stones face each other
in rows like booth-style
compartments in old trains.

Most of these people lived half
a mile from here and now they
couldn't be further away,

but they're all arranged as if
they're just trying to get home
and the train's waiting on a signal.

I walk between them, an inspector
in the aisles who has realised
all of his passengers are riding

with expired tickets
but is too scared
to call them all out.

THE FORK

When the invitation to a high school reunion
came to my door, I was on my knees
in the garden of our cul-de-sac home.

I was clearing a clogged gutter of dead leaves
and found that the best tool for the job
was a sharp-pronged Georgian cutlery fork
with a tapered deer antler handle.

I briefly thought of going, but then considered
the shame of having to account for what
I'd not become after showing such 'promise'.

When the Georgians made the fork long ago,
I imagine they never expected it would end up
here in my hand. Before them, it was the deer
that never expected to be whittled to a hilt.

MAC

Regardless of the gravity of the problem
I know that Mac, my sister's younger son
will seek out the help of any female
in the house, be they Grandma
or girl – and I love him for it.

Last Christmas I visited and ended up
in bed, depressed to hell. Mac wanted
to know what was wrong. *Nothing* I said.
He took my arm and before we got there
I knew he was leading me to my mother.

UNCLES

I went into the living room
to find one of my little nephews
scrubbing his arms with an eraser –
huge livid weals had formed.

I asked him what he was doing
and he said *I want*
to rub myself out
so I can be drawn again.

I said *It doesn't work like that*
and gave him a hug. Told him
about an Italian painter
who drew a perfect circle for a Pope.

You're that circle, I said. My sister
says he's having a tough time at school.
My uncles were both drunks.
They rubbed it out with drink.

OLD FRIENDS

Tom, John and I go out drunkenly,
aimlessly. We talk, laugh
and remember none of it.

We empty bottles to fill the day
and swim naked in the cold
meandering rivers of our lives.

Our love for each other
is three-legged, like a cracket
for milking that always finds its level.

Years of school and university
have taught us less than nothing.
But we know where the blackbird

likes to perch to sing
when the blackbird's
silent and not there.

APOLOGY

I bought this pen before I knew
what I would write
the way microscopes were made
before people knew
what they were looking for.

Ambulances only put their sirens on
if there's something in the way
and if I shouted at you then
it's because there's something
stopping me from getting to you.

All day I've thought about my actions
as I watched the fountain
desperately try to catch the self
it tossed away so nonchalantly
only seconds beforehand.

We never say what we mean
even when we mean it.

LIGNUM VITAE

I'm defensive, people say,
so I'm turning myself
into a Tudor warship.

Sparing no expense, I opt
for *lignum vitae* –
the tree of life.

So dense it grows
an inch to each
new generation of people.

Cannonballs can't touch it,
and so I launch it
on the world.

Down the causeway
it slips and as it touches
the water I remember,

it's the only wood
on earth
guaranteed to sink.

FATHER OF THE MAN

Sometimes I wish
I'd a forwarding address
for the person
I used to be,

to write to him
about the apples,
tired of waiting
to be picked, that fall

from the tree I planted.
Apples so red
they're ashamed or angry
not to have been the chosen ones.

SPELK

for David Coils (1964–2017)

You taught me woodwork
so you might expect me to take
your varnished oak kist
as my last memory of you.

I remember the music
at your funeral, the young piper
repeating the refrain
from Knopfler's 'Local Hero'.

It was far from the *Ceòl Mòr* –
but like pibroch, calculated
to have a little shudder in the drone
as someone walking over your grave.

It's when your body and voice
buckle with grief and all you let slip
is that tiny tremor, a mere spelk
for the seasoned carpenter.

FALLING

My Great Grandfather, Alfred Holden,
came from Felling and spent his life falling,

A reluctant corporal in the Border Regiment,
put on sniper-duty, he climbed a tree at Ypres.

Shot in the shoulder before he could take aim,
the fall saved his life, sent him home.

Later in a riveter's brace on the Tyne,
he plummeted into the bowels of a liner.

He worked hard to bring his family up a peg;
this made his drunken dive more spectacular.

They put him somewhere he could fall no more
but he'd already laced his gene pool

with a desire for descent. Sometimes I'm jerked
awake in the pitch middle of the night

by the feeling of free-fall. It used to scare me
but now I like the sense of weightlessness,

of being unburdened. Even the studio photo
of him taken on leave during the Great War

has a misty border to it, as if nowhere
and everywhere he's plunging through clouds.

BLUNT SAW

He's spent his life trying to conserve
old buildings and now he's falling apart
and there's no-one there to save him.

He once brought back an old church pew
from another church-turned-apartment-block.
It had to be cut down to size to fit in,

like a loss of religion, or a diminishing
congregation. He still believes in God,
though he's little faith in himself.

To slice the pew he took a blunt saw
and gashed his hand. You think blunt is safer,
but lower your guard and it wounds you worse.

Break

THE STAG

Takes time to keep things amicable.
We go on long country walks we once did
hand-in-hand and walk for miles together,
a metre apart, so soaked in our own pain

we barely notice a fallow deer stag, grazing
on nettles beside us. He looks in lofty pity
and carries on with his stinging repast.
We never married, I never was the stag

but this one's a saint for distracting us
briefly this awful day we walked to discuss
the killing of a love that, had it been a deer,
would have easily been a 16 pointer.

THE GIFT OF THE GAB

My party trick being able to talk
myself out of any sticky situation –
offences that would've had others
expelled merely saw me excused.

Convincing teachers the broken
window was the result of a fault
not my deliberately thrown stone.
The bullies seemed blind to me.

Police officers swept up my mess
and in Morocco I wormed my way
out of being mugged, even got
invited to my attacker's home for tea.

At home in even the roughest pubs,
I once talked my parents down
from divorce but I failed to change
your mind about leaving.

THE JOCKEY

A Scottish poet once told me
my surname 'McCaffery' is
a Gaelic patronymic meaning
'the son of the jockey'.

As a youngster I was good
at riding ponies and steeds
though I never really much
cared for the creatures.

You loved horses but sadly
they didn't love you back,
kicking and throwing you off
breaking your leg and coccyx.

In the months after you left
I imagine you as one
trying to get back in shape
after a long winter, losing

whatever weight you gained
to get fit for the race ahead,
even if that weight might be
me, the son of the jockey.

HIGH-LEVEL

The High-Level bridge, Newcastle to Gateshead –
the last time we crossed the river this way
we weren't sure if we were angry or moved
by all the lovers' padlocks – romantic barnacles
stuck to railings put up to stop suicides.

Today, New Year's Day, I walk it alone.
The council's cleared some of the padlocks
and I feel that from this vantage point –
the rusty concatenation of the bridges,
we've crossed some sort of Rubicon

and to others it appears as easy
as going over the High-Level.

THE FENCE

The Coquet between Warkworth to Amble
is a deceptively powerful tidal river.
The cable fence between water and footpath
was strong in the early days you visited
to see where I grew up. We walked here
and I made you laugh pretending to be
a jazz or metal bassist, strumming the wires.
I came this way today, the fence's in poor state,
one of the strands loose and wind-warped,
it looks like a cardiogram of my heart.

INVENTORY OF SCARS

Your skin is a map of where you've been
and it's tedious to boast scars but I must
have havered in harbour most of my life.

I've only two silvery cicatrices, on my thumb.
One gained as a pissed student slamming
a beer bottle on the bar and it shearing.

The other from a cheese cutter at a posh
party put on by my snobby ex-in-laws.
The scars are less than a centimetre apart –

one a watermark of the wild old me
who was nearly killed off by the other me,
trying too hard to fit in.

YESTERDAY'S NEWS

I know even this isn't the last time I'll sort
through that box of antique glasses.

We've moved them with us across three
countries, carefully packed with sheets

of whatever local newspaper came to hand.
We divide now instead of share between us

these breakables, swaddled in old headlines
in both Flemish and English.

This disaster won't make the tabloids
but I hope it reaches print here.

CONSERVATION

The village pub's a listed building
and I sit this late October watching
a dying wasp crawl the bullseye windows.

The last of its hive, perhaps. Gone
beyond harassing me for my beer,
it drifts feebly across the wobbly pane.

This soon to be dead survivor
was born in the month of our split,
when it dies we really are history.

This nuisance I once wanted to kill
I now desperately want to save.

BOOK TROUGH

Remember how you encouraged my bibliomania,
urged me to fill every room with old books?
We scoured car-boot sales for little wood troughs
to fit the tomes in every nook of our home.

Most of them were old school woodwork projects
but occasionally we snagged something better
like the teak one made from the timbers
of HMS Britannia, scrapped in Blyth, 1916.

There's a foxed etching of the ship being broken
which I saw years ago when we lived in Belgium.
Its ghostly prow a seagull picked ribcage.
Ships are always gendered female. I'm reminded

of how I put you through tempests and ended
washed up here, my things crammed in one room.

THE RING

I keep getting the same dreams
and wonder if you do too –

struggling to get the silver ring
I wore for 13 years off my finger

but it's swelling, the digit
like a lamb's elastic-banded tail.

Any head-doctor would tell me
it's about the difficulty of letting go,

realising it's over. I leave the ring
in a tin, the way people still keep

the milk teeth of their children
as if they'll ever need them again.

PERSONAL HARVEST

Land tilled since Roman times,
each age reflected in potsherds
the plough dredges up:
delft, willow pattern, Samian ware,
salt-glaze, clay-pipe and Bartmann.

It's both a horror and comfort
these fields yield almost the same
crops they did a thousand years ago,
the earth accepting what's broken,
saying *this will always happen.*

BAD FIT

All my life my body's been an enemy,
wearing clothes too tight to halt any gain,
suits unsuitable and shirts stifling me.

Just before you left me for good, I noticed
the Orcadian silver band you put on my finger
over a decade ago had kept that digit

thinner than the right-hand one, the skin
underneath incorrupt as a relic. It's been off
two months now and no longer fits at all.

I'm reminded of the lime tree I planted
in an old Belfast sink, the roots eventually
fumbling escape through the plug hole,

riveting the sink to earth at first,
then breaking it in two.

SANDCASTLES

Trust it to be glorious
weather the day I met you
on our favourite beach
for the post-mortem talk
about our failed relationship.

Sitting and talking in the dunes,
I began to dig a hole by hand
and as we reached some sort
of understanding I filled it back in
but am unsure even now

if it was a burial or exhumation,
a planting or reaping, or all four.

MOVING BACK

The first field is full of waist-high barley
pulsing in golden whiskery waves
and the second is recently ploughed
into vast clayey breakers.

This is my home, a constant that always
changes, flooded with summer's high tide.
What it is to stand on *terra firma*
and also feel so adrift on the sea.

TUAREG TENT-PEG

The only souvenir I wanted from Morocco
was a carved Tuareg tent-peg, eventually
found in a backstreet in Marrakech.

It looks like an ebonised Moorish cricket bat
but that's too Anglocentric. It might've
been cultural appropriation if it wasn't for

the fact that it's fake – no Moroccan lets
their heritage go like we Westerners do
to the first cash-waver. An expert told me

a self-respecting Berber would never carve
a peg on only one side. The patina comes
from street-shit, dirt, engine oil and cinders

caressed with spit and piss. Still I love it,
have moved it from home to home and back
again until at last the caravan's just myself.

BLAWEARIE

It means *tired of the wind*,
the name of the derelict farm
on the moors, built in the ruins
of a Bronze Age burial cairn.

We walked to it for the first time
in 2020. I've not been back since.
Remember the claggy tracks
covered in the hoof prints of sheep?

Like the thumb marks of potters
making a bowl for us to save
the memory of this day, should
the wind try to blow it away.

THE CRAB

He ran out along the broken breakwater
into the blue above, below and beyond

He thought of going underneath it all,
vanishing for good, so people might notice.

One desperate day he got to the sea,
set on throwing himself in, swimming

until legs or arms or lungs gave up
but the beauty of the place waylaid him.

From his vantage he saw a large crab
sidle from under a stone and back again,

vulnerable in the open only for a moment
like a thought had and thought better of.

AFTER THE STORM

came another storm, and then another,
seasons gave way to the song of chainsaws,
the cruelty and largesse of high water.

It left our most loved local character dead,
spared all the gravestones in the kirkyard
but felled the ancient living trees.

There was a hamper raffled for charity,
full of crap, sponsored by the undertakers,
their hearse drove by blasting a pop song.

People said the squalls were bailiffs
at their panes, how the wind sounded
like their lives being rewound on tape.

You could tell the truly faithful as those
who still travelled by public transport
and I recalled how it all began one night,

I was standing waiting for a lift, the lamp-
post and myself both being shaken. How
I felt love for something that can't feel love.

SERMON

In the churchyard the red admiral
lands on the wall where I'm sitting.

It perches with wings
closed in a namaste

but the wind keeps
prizing it open like pages

in a book before the spine's broken.
The stained glass of those wings

takes me into the church where
a bible with its hinges cracked

is spreadeagled on the lectern
at the same old passage.

My father attends service here.
I asked him what the sermon

he just sat through was all about.
He'd already forgotten. His brow

in a furrow until it came to him.
It was about joy.